RUDE WORDS

WORDS

Jake Harris

summersdale

THE LITTLE BOOK OF ESSENTIAL RUDE WORDS

Summersdale Publishers Ltd
46 West Street
Chichester
West Sussex
PO19 1RP
UK

www.summersdale.com

Printed and bound in Great Britain

ISBN: 1-84024-580-8
ISBN 13: 978-1-84024-580-6

THE LITTLE BOOK OF
ESSENTIAL
RUDE
WORDS

Introduction

The naughty, the nasty and the downright dirty – there's nothing quite like a rude word. With times a-changin' it's no longer considered a faux pas to drop 'shit' and 'bollocks' into a pleasant conversation with the grandparents; they'd probably consider it an insult if you didn't.

Even the words we used to prize for their dependable shock value have become more acceptable thanks to the loose lips of fashionable celebrities. Fucking cunts. But let us not be disheartened. Let us not forget how great it is to be truly offensive. May our potty mouths speak out and in one voice declare 'Fuck you!' to all those who would try to take away the beautiful gift of profanity.

Within the sweaty confines of this filthy little book you will find an inspiring collection of nasty words and equally offensive alternatives. Go forth and embrace your right to be rude and shit on anyone who tells you not to.

ARSEHOLE

BATTY HOLE

BROWN EYE

CACK PIPE

CHOCOLATE CANAL

CHOCOLATE STARFISH

ARSEHOLE

FART CHIMNEY

MARMITE CANYON

POOP SHOOT

RING PIECE

SHIT CREEK

ARSE-FUCK

BONE-SMUGGLE

BROWN LOVE

BUTT-FUCK

FUDGE-PACK

GO TO BROWN TOWN

GO UP THE OLD DIRT ROAD

ARSE-FUCK

GO GREEK

IGNITE THE RECTUM ROCKET

MARMITE-MINE

PLOUGH THE BACK FIELD

RIDE THE PONY

UP THE CRACK

BALLS

BOLLOCKS

CRACKERJACKS

FAMILY JEWELS

FIGS

GONADS

BALLS

HAPPY SACKS

KNACKERS

LOVE SPUDS

TWO VEG

BALL-SUCKING

BALL-BATHING

BATHING THE KIDS

GOB-STOPPING

EATING YOUR VEG

BALL-SUCKING

NUT-MUNCHING

SACK-SAMPLING

SWILLING THE SPHERES

TEA-BAGGING

TWINS' DAY OUT

BI

AMBISEXTROUS

**DIPS IT IN
BOTH PONDS**

DUNT

FLIP-FLOP

BI

GREEDY

LADY DI

LUCKY-DIPPER

PLAYING FOR BOTH TEAMS

BIG DICK

BEEF BAYONET

BIG WANG

CAPTAIN COCK

DONKEY DICK

MAN CANNON

BIG DICK

PORK SWORD

SCHLONG

THE HONOURABLE MEMBER FOR PANTINGTON

THE PYTHON

THIRD LEG

BIG TITS

AIR BAGS

BABYLONS

BAPS

BAZOOKAS

DIRTY PILLOWS

DUMPLINGS

FUN BAGS

BIG TITS

GLANDS FOR THE HANDS

KNOCKERS

LOVE CUSHIONS

MELONS

NORKS

UDDERS

BLOW YOUR LOAD

BLAST OFF

BUST A NUT

CREAM YOUR JEANS

POP YOUR CORK

RELEASE THE
TESTICULAR SQUATTERS

BLOW YOUR LOAD

SKEET

SPILL YOUR SEED

SPLATTER PLATTER

SPOOGE

SPREAD YOUR MAN MUSTARD

BOG

BOMB SITE

CRAPPER

DIRTY SOFA

DUMPING GROUND

BOG

GARY GLITTER

POO HOLE

POTTY

SMELLY THRONE

BUSH

BEAVER

DOWN THERE HAIR

FLUFFY CHALICE

FOLIAGE

FURRY FIELD

BUSH

LADY GARDEN

MUFF

RAT

SECRET GARDEN

SHRUB

CLIT

KIDNEY BEAN

KITTEN IN A CRADLE

LITTLE MAN IN A BOAT

LOVE SPOT

PEARL

CLIT

PLEASURE PATCH

RABBIT'S NOSE

ROLLER-BALL

THIRD NIPPLE

STUMP

CUM

ALBINO LOVE CHUTNEY

BABY BATTER

COCK CUSTARD

CUNT MAYO

FILTHY COCK VOMIT

JIZZ/JISM

LOAD

CUM

LOVE GOO

MAN GRAVY

POPULATION PASTE

SATAN'S EGG NOG

SEX WEE

SPUNK

CUM BATH

BUKKAKE

CREAM PIE

FACIAL

ICING

MUD PIE

CUM BATH

PEARL NECKLACE

RUNNY JACKET

SNOWSTORM

STICKY MOP JOB

CUNT

BEEF CURTAINS

BERKSHIRE HUNT

BLACK FOREST GATEAU

CLOWN'S POCKET

GASH

HAIRY AXE WOUND

HAIRY CLAM

HAM WALLET

CUNT

LOVE TUNNEL

MINGE

PROTECTED AREA OF OUTSTANDING NATURAL BEAUTY

QUIM

SLIT

SNATCH

TROUT MOUTH

WIZARD'S SLEEVE

DICK

COCK

CUNT TICKLER

DONG

JOHNSON

KNOB

LANCE CORPORAL

DICK

LOVE PUMP

LOVE TRUNCHEON

ONE-EYED TROUSER SNAKE

SALAMI

WILLY

DILDO

BILBO BAGGINS

COCK ON CALL

MANUAL MAN

PHALLIC FRIEND

DILDO

PLASTIC PAL

REPLACEMENT DICK

SEX STAND-IN

THE
HARD MAN

DRY CUNT

AUSTRALIAN BUSH

BARREN BEAVER

BRING YOUR OWN

DRIED UP CANAL

DRY CUNT

DUSTY DOORSTEP

FANNY FAMINE

HOSEPIPE BAN

LUBE-LESS

SAHARA SEX-TRAP

FART

ANAL SALUTE

BLOWING THE BUTT BUGLE

BOTTOM BURP

CHEEK FLAPPER

CUT THE CHEESE

FART

DEATH BREATH

GAS FROM THE ASS

RECTAL TREMOR

SHIT FUMES

FAT ARSE

ASSNORMOUS

BEASTY BUMPERS

FULL MOON

SADDLE BAGS

FAT ARSE

SPACE SHUTTLE LANDING SITE

TRUCK END

WIDE LOAD

FAT BASTARD

BAKERY BANDIT

BLOATER

DOUGH BOY

FATZILLA

FLABBA THE HUT

FAT BASTARD

LARD ARSE

**ONE DONUT SHY OF
HIS OWN POSTCODE**

PORKER

TUBBY TWAT

WIDE BOY

FAT BITCH

BEACHED WHALE

BEAST

BIG BONED

BLIMP

BLOB

FAT BITCH

FLAB HANDLE

HEFTY

POUND STRETCHER

STUFFED SAUSAGE CASING

FISTING

ANAL-PUNCHING

BEAKING

BUTT-BOXING

FIST-FUCKING

FOREARM FUN

FISTING

HANDBALL

HIGH FIVE

LENDING A HAND

TEN PIN BOWELING

FUCK!

ARSE!

BALLS!

BLOODY-HELL!

BOLLOCKS!

FUCK!

CRAP!

FECK!

FUCKING HELL!

SHIT!

FUCK OFF!

FUCK YOU FUCK FACE!

FUCK YOU MOTHER-FUCKER!

GET BENT!

GO FUCK YOURSELF!

FUCK OFF!

PISS OFF!

SCREW YOU!

SPIN ON IT!

UP YOURS!

GAY

ANAL BUCCANEER

BUM BANDIT

CHUTNEY FARMER

COCK COWBOY

COCOA SHUNTER

COLON CHOKER

FUDGE NUDGER

GAY

HAEMORRHOID HIT MAN

MUD JOUSTER

REAR ADMIRAL

RECTUM ROMEO

SAUSAGE JOCKEY

TURD BURGLAR

GIRL ON GIRL ACTION

CUNTATHON

CUNT ON CUNT

FINGER-LICKIN' FIESTA

LADY LOVIN'

GIRL ON GIRL ACTION

RIDE OF THE VAGERIES

SNATCH SALSA

THE QUIM PARADE

TITTY TANGO

HAND JOB

BUFF THE WAND

FINGER FUCK

FIVE KNUCKLE SHUFFLE

PLAY
THE
TROMBONE

RAISE THE FLAGPOLE

HAND JOB

SHAKE HANDS WITH THE PRESIDENT

TUG THE SAUSAGE

STROKING THE CAT

WEEDING THE GARDEN

HARD-ON

BONER

CLOTHES PROP

DRAW SWORD

DUKE OF THROBINGTON

FLESH ROCKET

FRANKENBONER

FULL MAST

HARD-ON

HIS MANLINESS

HORN

KNOB-ON

ROD OF STEEL

STIFFY

THROBBER

WOODY

HORNY

CHAMPING AT THE BIT

DOGGY

FIT TO BURST

FUCKISH

GAGGING FOR IT

HORNY

HOT

LIKE A RHINO

ON HEAT

RANDY

UP FOR LOVE

LESBIAN

BEAN FLICKER

CARPET MUNCHER

CLIT CARETAKER

LABIA LICKER

LESBIAN

MUFF DIVER

TACO EATER

VAGETARIAN

VULVA VULTURE

LIMP DICK

COCK DOWN

FALLEN SOLDIER

FLOPPY JOE

LAME RICHARD

LIMP DICK

MR FLOPPSIE

ONE MAN DOWN

STAGE FRIGHT

WET PUPPY

LITTLE DICK

ACORN

COCKTAIL SAUSAGE

GOLF PENCIL

MICRO MEMBER

LITTLE DICK

SUSPICIOUS PACKAGE

TEENY WEENY

WEE WILLY WINKY

WHERE'S WILLY?

LITTLE TITS

BEE STINGS

FLATLANDS

FRIED EGGS

MINI MILKS

NO-MAN'S-LAND

LITTLE TITS

PANCAKES

SATSUMAS

SMARTIES

SMUGGLED PEANUTS

MAN ON MAN

BEDKNOBS AND BROOMSTICKS

BUTT BANDIT MASSACRE

DICK DISCO

DICKS AT DAWN

MAN ON MAN

PENIS PARTY

SNOOKER

SWORDFIGHT

WILLY WORKOUT

MAN-WHORE

HAS A SLAPPERTITE

HIMBO

LIKE A DOG WITH TWO DICKS

MAN-WHORE

MUFF MASTER

PROSTIDUDE

SPERMINATOR

STUD MUFFIN

MINGER

BACK END OF A BUS

DOG

DOG ROUGH

**FELL OUT THE UGLY TREE
AND HIT EVERY BRANCH ON
THE WAY DOWN**

FUCK PIG

MUNTER

MINGER

PIG

ROTTER

ROUGH AS ARSEHOLES

TWO O'CLOCKER

UGGERS

MUFF DIVE

ATTEND TO PRINCESS LABIA

CARPET MUNCH

CLIT CLEAN

EAT A MCMUFF

FEAST FROM THE FURRY CUP

MUFF DIVE

GO FISHING

LICK THE PLATE

PEARL DIVE

POON DIP

TICKLE THE MOUSE

MUFF DIVER (TIME OF THE MONTH)

BLEEDIN' STEVEN

BLOOD SUCKER

CAPTAIN RED BEARD

CARNAL CANNIBAL

DIRTY DRACULA

MUFF DIVER (TIME OF THE MONTH)

LAD IN RED

LIPSTICK LOVER

PLACENTARIAN

RAW STEAK FEASTER

NICE ARSE

COMFY CUSHIONS

CUPCAKES

FUCK BUTT

NICE RIDE

NICE ARSE

PAIR OF CHERRIES

SEXY SADDLE

SWEET CHEEKS

TWO PEACHES IN A BLANKET

ORGY

COMMUNAL FUCKATHON

CROWDED HOUSE

FREE FUCKING FOR ALL

LOVE HUDDLE

ORGY

MUMMIES AND DADDIES

ONE BIG HUG

SNAKES
AND
FANNIES

**SPAGHETTI
JUNCTION**

PISS

BREAK THE SEAL

DO THE YELLOW RAIN DANCE

DRAIN THE LIZARD

HAVE A SLASH

PISS

GO FOR A WAZZ

SQUIRT THE DIRT

TAKE A LEAK

WATER THE PLANTS

PISSED

BATTERED

CRAPULOUS

CUNTED

FUCKED

LOADED

PISSED

RAT-ARSED

SHIT FACED

TWATTED

WANKERED

RIMMING

ARSE-KISSING

BACKYARD CLEAROUT

BROWN JOB

BROWN-NOSING

RIMMING

INVADING THE BORDER

LICKING THE TOILET SEAT

RIM JOB

RING-LICKING

SHAG

BEAVER HUNT WITH A SPEAR

BUTTER THE BREAD

CLEAN THE CARPET

DANCE THE HORIZONTAL TANGO

DIP YOUR WICK

DO THE NO PANTS DANCE

DO THE RUMPY PUMPY

SHAG

FILL THE CREAM DOUGHNUT

GET A SHOVE IN YOUR BLIND EYE

GIVE SOMEONE A HOT BEEF INJECTION

LAY THE PIPE

RIDE THE WILD BALONEY PONY

WORK THE HAIRY ORACLE

SHIT

CHOP OFF A GORILLA FINGER

CRAP

CURL ONE OUT

DO A BRAD PITT

DO A JOHN WOO

SHIT

DROP THE KIDS OFF AT THE POOL

PINCH A LOAF

TAKE A DUMP

UNLOAD

SLAG

COCKAHOLIC

DIRTY WHORE

FILTHY WENCH

HOSE BEAST

JIZZ BUNNY

SCRUBBER

SLAG

SKANK

SLAPPER

SLUT

STRUMPET

TRAMP

VILLAGE BICYCLE

WHORE

SUCK COCK

BLOW

CLEAN PIPE

CHOW DOWN

FACE FUCK

GAG ON A PYTHON

SUCK COCK

KISS THE WORM

PLAY THE PINK OBOE

SPIT POLISH

SUCK THE SAUSAGE

TEASE

BALL BREAKER

BITCH

CLIT TEASE

CUNT TEASE

TEASE

FUCK-WIT

HEAD FUCK

PRICK TEASE

TITTY TWISTER

THREESOME

CROWD

FRUIT BOWL

ONE-ON-TWO
SESSION

THREE AMIGOS

THREESOME

THREE MUFFKETEERS

TRIANGLE OF LOVE

TRIPLET PARTY

TRIPOD

THROW UP

BARF

BLOW CHUNKS

CHUCK

CHUNDA

HURL

THROW UP

MAKE AN OFFERING TO THE PORCELAIN GOD

SPEW

YAK

YAWN IN TECHNICOLOUR

TIT WANKING

BOOBY BUFFING

BUNNY RIDING

HOTDOGGING

JUG FUCKING

TIT WANKING

MAKING A SAUSAGE SARNIE

MELON MOWING

PILLOW PLOUGHING

WANKER

ARSEHOLE

BELL-END

COCK CHEESE

CUNT

DICKHEAD

WANKER

FUCK-WIT

KNOBHEAD

MOTHER-FUCKER

TOSSER

TWAT

WANKING FOR BOYS

BANGING ONE OUT

BASHING THE BISHOP

CHOKING THE CHICKEN

DATING PAMELA HANDERSON

DOING THE JEDI HAND TRICK

HAVING A HAND SHANDY

WANKING FOR BOYS

HAVING A TUG OF WAR WITH CYCLOPS

MUTILATING YOUR MUTTON

PLAYING POCKET BILLIARDS

SHAKING THREE TIMES MORE THAN A PISS

SLAPPING THE SALAMI

WANKING FOR GIRLS

**COMPOSING ON
THE SINGLE KEY PIANO**

DISTRESSING THE CRESS

DOING THE TWO
FINGER TACO TANGO

DOUBLE CLICKING YOUR MOUSE

FLICKING THE BEAN

FRIGGING

WANKING FOR GIRLS

GUSSET TYPING

HARVESTING LENTIL

IMPEACHING BUSH

MUFF BUFFING

POLISHING THE PEARL

RUBBIN' THE NUBBIN

SLAPPING
THE GASH

WATER SPORTS

BAPTISING

DETONATING THE YELLOW LASER BEAM

GOLDEN SHOWERS

SCAT SEX

SPLOSHING

WATER SPORTS

TOILET TRAINING

TURNING ON THE TINKLE

WARM RINSING

WETTING THE BED

WET CUNT

DRIPPING FOR IT

FIZZING AT THE SLIT

FROTHED UP

**HAIRY SANDWICH
WITH EXTRA MAYO**

WET CUNT

NIAGARA FALLS

RAINFOREST

SLIP 'N' SLIDE

SNAIL TRAIL

Eighteenth-century Rude Words

We may have invented 'fucking bitches' and 'dripping cunts' but the folk of yesteryear had a fair few ways of saying things to make the gentry blush.

Back in the 1700s, times were harder and lives were shorter. But that didn't stop our dear old ancestors using the time wisely and coming up with some essential rude words of their own.

Whether you're down the market calling the fruit-stall owner a sodomist, or showing off your scrotum to a local disease-infected hooker, these essential eighteenth-century words will give you something to shout about.

Never again will you feel out of place at your local colonial-themed brothel or on the set of *Eastenders*. Now get stuck in, you bracket-faced bufe nabber*.

*ugly dog catcher

EIGHTEENTH-CENTURY RUDE WORDS

APPLE DUMPLIN' SHOP

a woman's breasts

BACK GAMMON PLAYER

a sodomist

BEARD SPLITTER

a promiscuous man

EIGHTEENTH-CENTURY RUDE WORDS

BLOW THE GROUNSILS

to lie with a woman on the floor

BROTHER OF THE GUSSET

a pimp

BUCK FITCH

a lecherous old fellow

EIGHTEENTH-CENTURY RUDE WORDS

BUNTER
a low dirty whore/beggar

COCK ALLEY
a woman's genitalia

CODS
the scrotum

EIGHTEENTH-CENTURY RUDE WORDS

DOODLE SACK

a woman's genitalia

FETCH METTLE

masturbate

FIRE SHIP

a woman with venereal disease

EIGHTEENTH-CENTURY RUDE WORDS

GIMGAMBOBS

a man's testicles

LACED MUTTON

a prostitute

LOBCOCK

a large flaccid penis

EIGHTEENTH-CENTURY RUDE WORDS

MADGE

a woman's private parts

MUTTON MONGER

a compulsive womaniser

PEGO

the penis of a man or a beast

EIGHTEENTH-CENTURY RUDE WORDS

PEPPERED

infected with venereal disease

PUFF GUTS

a fat man

RANTALLION

one whose scrotum is so relaxed as to be longer than his penis

The Little Book of Essential Foreign Swear Words

Emma Burgess

£2.99

ISBN: 1 84024 239 6

ISBN 13: 978 1 84024 239 3

Ever been lost for words abroad?

Impress the world with a stream of multi-lingual profanity from this nifty pocket book.

Insulting new-found foreign friends has never been such fun!

www.summersdale.com